Blue Mother

Anja Mujić

Copyright © Anja Mujic, 2025
Published 2025 by The Book Reality Experience,
an imprint of Leschenault Press, Leschenault, Western Australia

ISBN: 9781923454330 - Paperback
ISBN: 9781923454347 - EBook Edition

All rights reserved. The right of Anja Mujic to be identified as author of this Work has been asserted by her in accordance with sections 77 and 78 of the Copyright, Designs and Patents Act 1988.

This book is a work of fiction and any resemblance to actual persons, living or dead, or locations, is purely coincidental. No part of this publication may be reproduced or transmitted in any form or by any means, electronic or mechanical, including photography, recording, or any information storage or retrieval system, without permission in writing from the publisher.

The author asserts that no Artificial Intelligence methods, techniques or tools have been used within the researching or production of this novel. Without in any way limiting the author's [and publisher's] exclusive rights under copyright, any use of this publication to "train" generative artificial intelligence (AI) technologies is expressly prohibited. The author reserves all rights to license uses of this work for generative AI training and development of machine learning language models.

Quotations & Permissions Notice
Every effort has been made to properly identify, credit, and where necessary obtain permission for the use of copyrighted material quoted within this work. Quotations are used in accordance with Fair Dealing provisions for the purposes of research, study, criticism, review, and reporting news. If you believe any material has been included in error or without appropriate acknowledgement, please contact the publisher in the first instance so that the matter may be addressed promptly.

Publisher: Leschenault Press, Email: legal@leschenaultpress.com

Cover Design by Brittany Wilson | Brittwilsonart.com

For my grandparents

Stanka, Enver, Živko, Džavida

Also by the author

love letters to places…

The temple bell stops—
But the sound keeps coming
out of the flowers.

— *Matsuo Bashō*

Contents

Restoran Vrbas 3

June Tanka (Ohrid) 6

Đurđevdan (Paleokastritsa) 7

Younger self on the Hauptstrasse (Heidelberg) 11

Deer Creek 13

The Carob Tree (Vis) 14

Aubade 18

18:47 (Pont des Arts) 20

Ethnography:

      In the distance, a fire burns on Pionirska 22

The Lexicon of Memory 26

two vignettes for mo(u)rning 29

I was   sorry   I would die thirsty 30

Sant'Agnello 37

Haibun As Family Portrait 38

Tur (Corfu) 42

Vietnam: A Retelling In Disorder 46
    i. The Life Cycle of an Oyster (Hue) 47
    ii. Portrait of Mai (Sa Pa) 48
    iii. Living with Ghosts (Hanoi) 49
    iv. The Foot Rowers of Tam Coc 50
    v. Hôi An 52

The Five Stages 55
Nikita and I (Cappadocia) 58
The Shape of a Morning Prayer (Istanbul) 60
Ghazal 61
Somewhere in the world, Kyoto exists 62
Renku (Tokyo) 63

Glossary, Notes & Acknowledgements 68
About the Author 72

I am the smallest among bodies lining the floor. The first breath of morning swells, magenta bruises forming on the window glass. Around me, the rhythm of dreams alternates; fruitless branches swaying inside the room's blueish walls, greyed with lack of light, as if foreshadowing. To some, we are in the White City. To others, we are playing house in the hornet's nest. To me, we are whatever war makes of us. The frenzied arms of the wooden conductor continue to flail inside the walls, shadowed hands striking air, the wail of cut gourds ricocheting through the emptiness, as if to harness it. Years from now, in the wilderness of a distant country, I'll meet a lone fawn frozen in the clearing, the air pierced thin with fear between us, and understand everything. Which is to say, we all survive by playing our parts. Under my mattress, copper threads weave meridians in the carpet; the sea we've been traversing stitching itself to the room's edge and soon, they say, to another place. Before the fight broke out, my mother had been reading me a story. She said, *we'll fly this time, so high, baby, like migrating birds casting southern skies*— the first breath of spring swelling magenta at her temple, a sunset. I want to hear again about Gulliver washing up on Lilliput, bewildered and motionless, but I can't remember anything before the pages burned. Somewhere, in that same distance, curled limbs imprint a meadow. The smallest among bodies lining the floor.

- Belgrade

Restoran Vrbas

I sit across my aunt at a restaurant on the edge

of the river, an emerald slipped into a pocket

of darkness, in which I had thrown a pumpkin

earlier. A witch from the Caribbean

told me the spell to break

a love curse. The waiter brings

a schnitzel that is a whole bird

minced, its bones destined for garden dust,

beak and claws carved for good

fortune, swimming in yolk

thickened with flour, golden

bread crumbs and a generous sprinkling of salt.

I think back to the first chicken I ever saw;

thrashing around a bathtub, my grandfather's

hands wrapped around its neck, feathers

and the smell of death

filling the air. His sleeves rolled up to the elbow

so as not to spoil the pressed white cotton

starched together with lace for Sunday lunch,

and how those same hands fed me

love and violence, a simultaneous root

forming. How it was understood

that one could not exist without the other.

I ask my aunt how she met my uncle.

She says he saw her and decided.

Out of the corner of my eye

I spot the winter

moon, pale and fading above the river

swelling rapidly— ancestors accelerating

to the crux of it. A few years later

my uncle died in a car crash and I wondered

if the women in this family are cursed

or rather blessed

with something that cannot be

harnessed. I think of my pumpkin

in the chokehold

of a log in the neighbouring town

fighting to go on. The waiter begins

to pack my plate. Leftovers

for days, he says. I feel the air shift.

My grandmother reminds me

never to eat chicken on New Year's Eve.

I check for patterns in the dirt

and in the sky, searching

blindly for Spring.

June Tanka (Ohrid)

i. Roadside fire swells

into the lake, June poppies

mirror solstice—

Shattered jewels through liminal sky,

spirits roll their vengeful dice.

    ii. Pulsing amber hands

    the dog-shaped omens, an orb

    illuminating dusk;

    Time drifts in slow motion,

    hills alight with clairvoyance.

        iii. Parched horizon veins

        the yolk of distant mountains

        drowsed on shallow air,

        pilgrim lays an ear to tomb—

        broken echoes of a saint.

Đurđevdan (Paleokastritsa)

At the edge of her knife, the body of Christ rises

with a sigh. She fashions the dough

into a braid around the rim

where the priest pours

wine, gushing molten into open mouths—

fertile vines and buds like baby's cheeks

descend in a dazzle

of bells. To the town below

time long dissolved the hero's passage;

Odysseus cast in petrified turquoise, his Phaecian love

forgotten.

After she's cut and quartered the rounds of yeast,
she carves the offering, her daughters gathered

to bathe in the river, their spring-washed hair adorned
with blooms and sprigs of rose-

mary, to slit the lamb's throat,
boiled wheat mounding like freshly dug earth in her hands

smashed figurines tracing sacrifice.
At the table, the priest pounds his fist to open

flame, his bejewelled knuckle etching the image of a Saint
in wax, he immortalises her infant. The fifth of too many

mouths agape in reverence. The feast undone,
grandmother takes her last breath,

the break of day dissolving on the concrete with a hiss,

a silk veil brought to shroud her Spirit. I come to kiss

the Saints' mosaiced lips, leave

a talisman in the well of the monastery. We break

bread as if cursed, still

gather thistle to bless a single drop.[1]

───────────────────────────

[1] Sheltering from lashings of bullet rain,

woodland treaties between three

orphaned siblings are twined with posy stems

and handshake spit. Plum stained

petals veil the river star-crossed lovers bathe in

generations later. Weeping

───────────────────────────

        willow lined bank marks time; Resilient

           harvests reap bitter fruit; barren

           reflections mirror droplets, golden

        casings (like promises) scatter the earth.

Younger self on the Hauptstrasse (Heidelberg)

> *Tomorrow doesn't exist. This moment*
>
> *Alone is mine, and I am only who*
>
> *Exists in this instant, which might be the last*
>
> *Of the self I pretend to be.*

— *Ricardo Reis*

I watch my younger self on the Hauptstrasse;

a stranger holding the softening blade

of winter crinkling inside her

hands, golden as if unwrapping

the sun. A carousel horse all sinew and spirit,

lazuli eyes pluming for the haze of blue

mountain ranges. Below the Neckar

sheds its skin, cracked grey as a misplaced Juniper

finding new ways to open. I remind her

how the fruit bats would swarm

the Southern sky without warning, inkless

hour; time with no mercy,

the tableau cracked—

Deer Creek

At Deer Creek, trees filter light

as if the world is ending. Engulfed

in oppressive heat and relentless

cicada song. Pink lizard tongues

and placid leech bodies hang

unsatisfied. Eucalyptus trees play

host to moths— scribbly gum letters

on ashen bark. Old fire lines the path

to shallows rippling over iron

ore— a shot deer bleeding out. Two

pink tongues get close but never

touch. In this light,

sand becomes snow; fool's gold

forecasts a lonely summer.

The Carob Tree (Vis)

When the carob tree flowers

    autumn shivers

along the nape, ridged and cat-kin

    like. Flesh

wraps branch bodies; two snake roots

    pausing to drink

full bellied in the sea in slow, deep gulps

    of salt.

And in the sky, a sliver

    of crescent grows

in the rhythm of an urchin

    lying on a ledge, rusted and slippery.

When the carob tree flowers, sweet

    pods drop to the earth

with a fat wet thump

    and the seed of two lovers

is surrounded by blue.

A madrigal blares through the window; the descent of skylarks floods our cathedral with unavoidable religion. I awaken gasping for light, internal organ working overtime. Next to me, his body is sculpted, where the Seine splits to open a sapphire eye. We counted constellations to pass the night, the weight of slow pilgrims collapsing on the horizon. Earlier, we were stone-faced, the Medusa-headed door folding in on us, life fading from Rue de Lancry. Now it's the beginning again, and a city has never been so quiet. I make my way to the fifth— a landscape of livid zinc as far as the eye can see, a violent vestige. Bottle green shards spattering messages on every ceiling. I close. I open. I ask the word for golden, a silent manifestation. In a split second, summer is gone, transfigured wisteria hanging where his hands had been. The night drenched in astronomical hues at my feet.

- Paris

-

Aubade

In the Jardin du Luxembourg

        night holds

        til the very last

breath, impaled

on fields of nakedness. Lavender

        ash lines

        the city slick

lips shape a gunshot

ringing. Somewhere

        in gossamer memory, we are the opposite

        of prey. Walk fast

through dawn   light

        breaks,

        Destiny shows

her face, made us believers

once. Remember how

                         we died

                         and how

our little deaths ricocheted

into morning the size of two weeks

                or two years

       or here we are

here we are,   still.

18:47 (Pont des Arts)

For Plavo Nebo

The sky is open   tonight

    Wounded. Winged

        scalpel folds it;

            meticulous flag

of blue,

    white, and red.   Somewhere,   the echo

   `   of a star. A swallow

        feather reminds me

of a story,

    father.

        Of a man who named his son

            after it,   then blew

the dusk through

    his mouth-opened nation—

        the pianist strikes

            moonrise,   an eye

half open.   Grey

    matter rains

        over the Seine.

Ethnography: In the distance, a fire burns on Pionirska

1992, Višegrad: 70 civilians are locked in a room and set on fire;
Generations of smoke. An abandoned garden. A bed of ashes lining
the porch.

2010, Lake Peruiac is emptied for dam repair;
A child's bones in a bag. Half a kilo of gold woven into cotton. An
amulet / a rope. A lipstick. A comb.

2015, Paris: Canal Saint-Martin is drained for cleaning;
A flammable rug. A fire extinguisher discarded by a street sign.
A 75mm shell. At least one gun.

2022, Paris: The city aflame as if it wants

to be beautiful. Someone I kissed

yesterday hangs

from the window frame, outheld

                hands sifting the season's

                      ashes

into cigarette embers,

into honey

            on the skin of pulped pomegranates

            littering the canal, a loose fingernail reflects

the swan swooping to drink

its nectar dripping

                dripping into sawdust,

                we speak the same language

in the country of flesh;

the weighted sigh of my mother

                    pulls through me as shrapnel

                                    pulls through rust

of the hour carved

into the sky by a bullet.

                                    By the window

                                            his silhouette

a singed wingspan, tells me

about a daughter

                                    who lives, I tell him

                                            I struck the match

knowing the flames could never contain us

but how a burnt-out Icarus is still

                                    more beautiful than any

                                            constellation—

"Athletes will swim in the Seine

during the 2024 Olympics

                                despite concerns of E. coli and bacteria"

                       "The reservist was upset that children swam

while officials remained silent

about the bodies concealed"

                                       Tendrils unfold into heat

                                 on the riverbed, we excavate

memory, a mute. Morning

shimmering tourmaline between us.

The Lexicon of Memory

On stage, a jazz trio croons

in a language

I've never heard. Bare bones sketch the city's

mountainous distance;

a glittering skeleton in the early winter

darkness. I flip

my cup and watch the sediments

intersect. Tasseography—

a dialect interpreted

with the fingertips. *Pipati*.

In a mother tongue. I think

of the fortune-teller who grabbed my *dlan*

on Torstrasse;

scanning its curved horizons, piercing

the flesh with promise

of *Smrt*. Do words carry more when they're

understood? I remember

the first dregs of English I ever learnt;

apple and apologise. Which is to say it

started with nourishment and forgiveness.

Which is to say

I was six and perfect

standing wide-eyed at the gateway of syntax,

ready to be corrupted

with absolution. On the train, I traced

the Balearic on one side

Parc del Garraf

on the other, finger moist

on the cold window, terrain destined for

pilgrimage.

Sjever, Istok, Jug, Zapad.

A traveller's prayer. I was nowhere

near. My merchant

Grandfather travelled the world. Somewhere

in the past, a young boy collects his absences.

Recites the itinerary

like a pledge

when I ask him. His voice on the other end

of an old telephone. Crack crack crack.

Tongue, a dud

missile. The silence of my youth littered

with fragments. I switch

tea for gin and think of the similarities

between

dug and *duh*. Someone

next to me stirs the fire. I come

back. Sculpt myself

out of vernacular. *Where are you from?*

A wet mouth. If you ever find yourself

inside it, remember that *gdje si* means where are you, but asks *how*

you are. *Tu sam.* Which is to say,

to be is inherently good.

two vignettes for mo(u)rning

/ sitges

how we ran / the shore / into / our lives / billowed / into /
engine smoke / our burnt soles / weeping / have you had
enough / the waitress pantomimes / granular lineage / sinking
/ into quick sand / how we hid / our religion / tightly bound
parasols / lining / the cliffedge / how we folded / into winter
/ white washed / tables / emptied / like the plastic / ones / we
ate from / those first years / a gift / from the salvation / army
/ how we were / white / enough / to be / gifted / salvation /
bismillah / how fear turned / father's teeth / to rain / drops /
the fisherman / tipping / his ashes / into / the sea / a hermit's
brush stroke / how God carves an eye / into / the storm / and
how / the storm is / an arrow

day begins / a slow burn / under / the skin / sun-curtain /
peeling / bodies / undressing / fruit / how / unencumbered /
hands / fold / in prayer / how / a rosebud / below / the basin
cups / memory / and how / the river / is the shape / of an
emerald / how / hypnotic / the Muezzin / calls / to beckoning
/ how light is / a prism / blossoming / on the Tekija / window
/ sill / overflowing / in unison / how / the dervish / whirls /
shadows / into ecstasy / his silhouette / calcified / his palms /
a conduit / how / the mountain / soil is porous / soaked / in
iron / but how / a blue / sky isn't / about / remembering /
how / it stays / above / how it splits / to open

/ blagaj

        I was   sorry   I would die thirsty

Distant graves are exchanging curses with closer ones.

- *Ivo Andrić*

1.

               Can you hear me?
                  say   yes

feel

                          if you can't
        I'll remind you
      Do you recall

                             father

       the woods
     fear
       breakthrough
         how you gave
  the night

                       where
                 surrender

  wounded
   where

2.

                            rifle
           told us
     to lay
everything
blue
               death   written
                     our hands up
   It sounds ironic   execution
       can you recall

3.

                    the grass
flattened
                    people
              gathered   the meadow,
      surrounded
   We
are from
Actually,

4.

  pistol in
  hand   searched
          nape of   neck

```
                as if
faces     buried
      didn't                         know
      time
           Long live
                      a man shooting
```

5.

```
      body
      numb         feel
                          water, somebody,
                            rifle
                      jerrycan            bottle
                                     a drop or two
            open     mouth
        rifle                         rifle
         rifle               rifle
                 through the canvas
                              children riding
      bicycles
                      people watching
          Witness
                           Drina
```

6.

                                      a relative
                still conscious,   people   walking
on top of him
                                            Do you know
me?   Yes, I know you, brother

7.

               give   up
be saved
                       We are
    somewhere
                                drinking
       darkness

8.

    clothes
    on the floor
                               feel
          time
Remember   will finish you

9.

entrance
             shot
 recognised a teacher
                      macadam road
       Is
      that you, sir?   Yes, it's me
                              it sounded like rain
                              gunfire

10.

I was   sorry   I would die thirsty

              to live

                              hurt

                                        sense it
                              mother
where

11.

water
     emerged
 river

                              of bodies

                    2

          3
                                              4
                     5

                            6
                      7
                8
                                         9
                                              10

---

[2] As a result of the war in Former Yugoslavia, 1600 clandestine gravesites were dug across the region

[3] They hid the bodies of approximately 30,000 people killed between 1991 and 1999

[4] The 42 largest sites contained the bones of over 10,000

[5] 456 exhumed bodies were children

[6] 94 of these sites are linked to the 1995 Genocide of the Bosnian Muslim population of Srebrenica

[7] Only 12 have been memorialised

[8] 12,000 people remain missing

[9] An Erasure Poem based on the Testimony of Witness O

[10] Dedicated to the victims and survivors of Genocidal Violence

Sant'Agnello

The scent of sinew lingers, sharp

and a little wet. I finger the rind;

outer grooves, premonitive pulp.

At the same time, I lie

on the remnants of eruption—

Vesuvian dust rakes my bones

into submission. I begin to peel

a tangerine in my hand, sometimes

alone, sometimes with another.

Haibun As Family Portrait

He stands in the hallway, arms extended to the altar of light. Illuminated particles shatter like snow around him as if a globe contained the image. In his hands, the vulnerable hues of a bruised newborn glow translucent, neon polymer to mark the night's offering. He inspects the notes before returning the pile to his pocket, carefully folding each fortune. At the airport, he slept on plastic somewhere between countries, nothing but a tattered briefcase clutched in his arms. As he drifts towards sleep again, the weight of his nod sets off an explosion, the tunnel bursting open into the harbour. The city limits shred long into the night and the night, long into itself. A makeshift priest on wheels, he spins drunken confessions into new beginnings. On the cusp of morning, he is awoken by a silver flash in the back seat. The woman's fare glimmering, something counterfeit in his hands.

-

Then the highway merged

into darkness, the horizon line fading

from pink to black, all roads leading inwards—

we had been on the road for years.

-

A red-eyed Grebe skids the distance of the Bogey Hole, back and forth, back and forth. The ghost of a river trout watches on in confusion, its blood-crusted gills thrashing for air. Everyone says we could easily drown in this new reckoning, but every day I watch you walk across oceans. Back and forth, back and forth. I wear my swimmers under my clothes at all times, strands of sun-kissed straw poking out from under rubber like an alter ego, goggles folded awkwardly in my pocket, just in case. In the garage, buoys of cabbage float in barrel-contained water in preparation for a winter that will never come. Back and forth, back and forth. The sulphuric scent seeps through the cracks.

-

We are riding in circles around the island. Red vans circling like tropical birds overhead. We are riding in circles around the island. *You're running, aren't you?* An old friend greets him. We are riding in circles around the island. The evergreen crowns of Aleppo Pines engulf our path. We are riding in circles around the island. Locks of my hair like seaweed wrapped around his fingers as he drags his fists along the sea floor. We are riding in circles around the island. The water so crisp I salivate. We are riding in circles around the island. There are allegations that the soil tastes metallic. We are riding in circles around the island. And that for seven years Calypso bent the will of her lover. We are riding in circles around the island. There are talks of a new hotel and day spa. We are riding in circles around the island. Where women were once prophets outside their bodies. We are riding in circles around the island. And rows of men-shaped beggars gathered to receive. We are riding in circles around the island. Boots against temples. We are riding in circles around the island. Our eyes closed, our hands free.

—

The air is rotten with the smell of brandy. A drop of it sits on the tip of a drunk's tongue, shimmering bronze in the sun's merciless flare. As he rambles on, the Fiat swerves to avoid potholes littering the highway like inverted stars, an erratic flame, not even the sacks of flour daring to breathe in the back seat. Ten hours. Forty-one checkpoints. Unspoken bullets scattering the highway. No guarantee we'd make it anywhere past ourselves. Somewhere along the way, the body begins to eat itself. Each hour, the price for a kilo of flesh. Teeth start to fall, like raindrops. The fear can no longer contain itself. A stretch of breath from where the Gazela splits the city, he stops and tells me to walk on as if I'm worthy of living. In a well-pressed suit and with a snappy briefcase. That if a soldier yells stop and the bullet misses, to drop and roll into the river. To swim as fast as possible towards the furthest reckoning. As children, we would swing from old tyres, shrieking with joy as our bodies broke the river's sugary surface. In near-death, the body remembers this joy. In life, this joy is the price for what the body remembers.

—

Honey oozes from cracked glass, coating a leather purse and all ten cartons of cigarettes with a liquid glow. Each cigarette is split between three men crouching in the dark. Grains of sugar lay disguised as bejewelled dirt at our feet. Red petals from the bridal bouquet fall through the air in slow motion, landing on the floorboard like sadness remembering. Behind them, dried tea leaves crunch between pages. Thistle and sage from the selo burn through bound memories. Something slain has been vacuum sealed and slotted in the folds of a suitcase, its flesh blessed with the absence of wrongdoing. In the back seat, someone's husband fingers the arm band ripped from the jacket of a dead soldier. A souvenir. A boy under a blanket. A lock of hair in a velvet jewellery box sits in his pocket. A family heirloom. The shine of shrapnel has been distributed among limbs, inconspicuous talismans. Broken parts of a doll are held together for most of the journey. A crescent moon face. A handful of teeth. A pearl necklace. Eyes blink beads of sweat in the rearview. We pass through the checkpoint unnoticed. Out the window, the leaves change.

-

We pass ourselves through

each other, like seasons

we are reborn.

Tur (Corfu)

The evening was at once intimate and infinite.

— *Jorge Luis Borges*

It was almost over when I saw him

the day, that is, through the cornfield unblinking—

two rubies refracting

a tunnel of light. An apparition;

his best evening coat making a mirror

out of us as if we were

split

from the same shadow. I fold

into the sonata of his ribs. The maiden

searching for his shape

in the Pleiades,

bathing her wishbone in butter

and yolk.

Dripping from his horns— blood

to grapevine,

her pulse transmitting

into the moment of my body.

As if to say;

here, take it. The day, that is,

an untamed constellation

swelling in the sky.

I carried morning on my back, a pulse with no body, only the radio finding its frequency. Surya balancing one legged on the dash, her elegant head bobbing in time. In the sky, feverish Deities spread quickly— hooves drumming the skin of dawn to climax. Among them, they carried a cluster of ruins, the soul long gone. A sickle slicing in vain through the flooded March fields, the mother's wail ringing out, more animal than human. The driver blowing incantations in the rearview, temple smoke billowing as the procession cleared.

- Mỹ Sơn

Vietnam: A Retelling In Disorder

i. The Life Cycle of an Oyster (Hue)

Bodies float unbothered in their suspended reality. From the roadside hammock, an impossible heat ribbons the highway into Hue. Surrender. Surrender. Surrender. In leatherbound hands, the bodies yield like unfolding moons, pried open by the blades of unravelling years. Sometimes gentle. Sometimes a whirlwind. The farmers don't seem to notice the broken-down taxi and newfound spectator. A toothless grin hands me an unnamed drink in a bright orange can, and the rest of the day boxed up in incense—a cigarette hanging from a vowel, a single glimmer of gold in the void. I had dreamt of being there already. Which is to say, it was the kind of heat to live for. So parallel to my own life.

ii. Portrait of Mai (Sa Pa)

I thought of Mai long after her sweet face faded into the Fansipan fog, dystopian against Sa Pa's new world skyline. As the masterfully loaded Yamaha sputtered at the thought of carrying us back down the mountain. How inevitably fearless she had become at such a young age, but how her inherent fire remained. How she was already a mother, her own eyes still welling with innocence. How sturdy she was, navigating the land every part her equal with simultaneous poise and command; sinking into oversized gumboots, a frail umbrella at her side, her tiny frame pulling me out of mounds of buffalo shit at every upward step. I can still smell it. How it is women like her who keep the soft threads of this merciless earth weaving, their sacrifices lining the path women like me stand on. How ashamed she made me. And how I yearned for a life that would show the sameness between us.

iii. Living with Ghosts (Hanoi)

For days, the city wept. Did you feel it coming? Outside the hotel, a small boy squats in the gutter playing with spilt tapioca pearls, his tiny fingers assembling to slug the bulging matter down the drain. Dream on the edge of it? Droplets fall in succession onto the surface of Hoàn Kiême lake, the cracked slate suddenly saturated with life. Did the warning stir you? At the temple centre, a calligrapher sits between two orange trees potted deep into earth red clay— *Anything you want*, with lightning at his fingertips. Was it elastic? The haunting wail of the Đàn Nhị laced with a distantly pervasive techno beat. Destabilising? I hear the crowds lining train street in anticipation, bloodthirsty. Was there surrender? The same canon of chaos and peace that made it impossible for the coroner to pin down the exact moment of rupture. Was there stillness? Time in Hanoi passes.

iv. The Foot Rowers of Tam Coc

"Keep your eyes on the river."

Reclining in a reverie, his elegant legs transform into wingspans.

"Why keep looking to where you've been?"

First across borders nobody was sure had opened, retracing the steps of a vague plan made in the days of the living.

"Do you mind?"

Locals line the riverbank to watch this duet. A woman joins. The rhythm remains unchanged.

"Limestone"

Lips gleam milk-white and swollen, a language rippling between them.

Silence.

Listening to the shrill of birdsong scraping against the eye of a giant—

"Something for me?"

He doesn't move. A Banyan begins

"Just one more look"

to hum, its wispy finger drawing a circle. A single spotlight

"We go under now."

of iridescence. Opens to the touch— old death by now a simple soil.

v. Hôi An

For my grandfather

When the old man rises, he makes his way to the wire coop at the bottom of the hill, squatting to reach for the still-warm eggs beneath each tuft of feathers. He then proceeds to check the barns full of swinging udders still grazing in their sleep, full of milk to be collected for his wife's cheese. Then the pigs, busy at their trough, getting big enough to tear the hands off a child. He continues wearing down the stone path with this routine, as he has done every morning for many years. Eventually, he finds his way to the roots of the village's oldest tree, where he kneels to listen, his ear pressed to the soil's scar tissue. By the river, women have begun to open the day with a song. One by one, joining the unplanned chorus. At their feet, children play games they seem way too young for. Solemnly, the men sit around, still discussing the war in each other's eyes. *We're still talking about the war,* my mother complains. Done with his rounds, the old man settles onto the porch of a house the colour of marigolds, looking out at last night's lanterns still burning fuchsia on the surface of the Thu Bôn. I watch his image fade into the ghostly flames reflected on the Colonial facade. An open–palmed child at my side; an opium seed crushed to abate our hunger.

Blame it or praise it, there is no denying the wild horse in us.

—Virginia Woolf

Dawn stretches the dough of our bodies into happiness, covering the circumference of the table, a thin white thread on the horizon. She begins with Fajr. I start with Surya Namaskar A and B. Side by side, we perform our prescribed rituals: standing, folding, and prostrating. She purifies with whispered words, I purify with whispered breath. After we pray, we break our fast with dates sweet enough to shatter the night, the ripe apple of her pisiform rising as she rubs it with tiger balm. She tells me how a bucking horse will shatter the fragile innards of a man; her father, my great-grandfather, generations that could not be held nor contained. Steam rises from the copper coffee pot. The table is laid with two porcelain cups and a special dish for sugar cubes. She passes me the flame, so close to her God in the end.

- Zenica

The Five Stages

1. Eibsee

First the space must sink

through the bones, return to earth

look back on itself.

2. Ölüdeniz

Foaming at the mouth,

hints of light ornament

the turquoise lagoon.

3. Ölüdeniz

Shimmering November

feet like shooting stars—

the paragliders land.

4. Tangier

Gutted cantaloupe

abandoned on the table

at golden hour.

5. Tangier

Locals drink, the day

a forced blessing, the city

burning to rapture.

Nikita and I (Cappadocia)

A valley of swords cut the sun

until it bled. Until red became

merciless; a valley of roses.

And heat turned to honey.

We made our way through

fear and trust; two beasts

demanding freedom,

without knowing the rhythm

of surrender.

If you tell a horse not to run

does it eventually forget?

Nikita shook her head

until memory conjured

a path of polished edges—

an untrustworthy smoothness.

In another life, we rode bareback

and the land was not so thirsty,

the sky burned instead of blue.

The Shape of a Morning Prayer (Istanbul)

Sun-laced lavender drips

through stained glass

and through me

like eternal sleep

I am awake to witness.

A thousand domes divulging

celestial ancestries

I'll never know.

The complex geometry

of my life

light-soaked on the Sahn.

A single taste

of ablution drips

down worn down stone

in timing divine

to its own specificity.

Ghazal

Silver pages soak in the dawn of your memory,
wrinkled with touch, verses lay drawn by your memory.

Light through the window embroiders the daisies on silk
to sweeten my chest with the scent of your memory.

Bodies fold to the embrace of their deities, sun
worship eternally adorned by your memory.

The weight of refrain is intoxicating, no time
lapsed or seas diminished could mourn like your memory.

No plane or train or season changed could give back the
milk and honey, the lingering thorn of your memory.

Ghostly hand on heart squeezes nectar from the flower
now swollen with the passing storm of your memory.

Somewhere in the world, Kyoto exists

where I am not and it is always

snowing, an individual carries firewood.

Everyone I meet absorbs my rage;

malleable mirrors with the softness of spring,

Sakura at the feet of rivers. I am soothed

into submission. A fig is slurped straight

from its branch in Dubrovnik, the scent

of late August, an aphrodisiac. Everywhere

exists where I am not, and if I can't be

in Kyoto, I'll be here. Making space for another

is softening the way Kyoto does.

From now on, I'll take my rain with traces.

Don't ask about the missing ingredient,

just tell me where the sky opens.

Warblers cheer the heron's migration. Two

individuals carrying firewood strike a match.

Somewhere in the world, Kyoto exists.

Renku (Tokyo)

Blossoms glisten

on the pavement like sugar

crystals in lover's hands.

Temple smoke billows,

fortune folded in my pocket.

Train tracks split—

crosswalk choreography;

empire state of mind.

Towering beauty

where night sky begins.

Atomic moon strokes

a glass xylophone,

the river shatters.

Into light, mask of day slips;

fanfare.

A mother walks where tendrils once caressed her feet. Scaling the ledge of a windowless frame, the city swells beneath her; a bruise of Jacaranda healing against the sky. Inside the room there is only one suitcase. One suitcase for four lives. Deep in thought, her fingertips trace the scattered relics. First, the documents, the photographs, the jewellery. Then the clothes and embroideries. The frays of a land she once knew. She thinks about breaking and how everything is light. In the distance, the shape of a body beckons, endless and blue.

- Epilogue

Glossary, Notes & Acknowledgements

The book's epigraph is a translation by Robert Bly from The Sea and the Honey Comb: A Book of Tiny Poems, 1971, Beacon Press.

The book's opening prelude was first published under the title Belgrade in Collateral Journal Vol. 10.1, 2025.

Đurđevdan (Paleokastritsa): It is estimated that between 1941 and 1945, the Nazi backed Ustaše regime murdered up to 500,000 Serbs, expelled a further 300,000, and subjected at least 200,000 to forcible conversion. This piece is dedicated to my maternal grandparents, both made orphans by this violence.

The epigraph on page 9 is by Ricardo Reis, one of the heteronyms created by Portuguese poet Fernando Pessoa. The translation by Richard Zenith is from A Little Larger Than The Entire Universe, Selected Poems, Penguin Publishing Group, 2006.

Deer Creek was first published in Humana Obscura Issue 9, summer 2024.

The Lexicon of Memory:

Pipati: To touch, grope, feel

Dlan: Palm

Smrt: Death

Sjever, Jug, Istok, Zapad: North, South, East, West

Dug: Debt

Duh: Ghost or Spirit

Ethnography: In the distance, a fire burns on Pionirska: The details referenced at the start of this piece are inspired by the articles of Marta Vidal for Balkan Diskurs 2016, Hikmet Karčić for Balkan Insight 2023, and Angelique Chrisafis for The Guardian 2016.

Witness O (whose name and identity have been withheld from public knowledge) is a survivor of the Srebrenica Genocide. I was sorry I would die thirsty is an erasure poem based on the English translation of the transcript of their testimony given to the International Criminal Tribunal for the Former Yugoslavia on 13 April 2000, in the case against Radislav Krstić. The statistical data mentioned in the piece is courtesy of Balkan Insight. The epigraph for this piece (on page 26) is by Ivo Andrić from the English edition of The Bridge on the Drina, translated by Lovett F. Edwards, University of Chicago Press, 1977.

An iteration of Sant'Agnello was first published as Plasticine Tangerine in Visual Verse Anthology VOL. 08 ~ CHAPTER 11.

Haibun as Family Portrait:

Selo: Village

On page 38, the line "I fold into the sonata of his ribs" is after Ocean Vuong. The epigraph for this piece is from The Book of Imaginary Beings, translated by Norman Thomas di Giovanni in collaboration with Jorge Luis Borges and Margarita Guerrero, Penguin Books, 1974.

An iteration of Vietnam, A Retelling in Disorder, was first published for the 2022 Born Writers' Award Shortlist.

The epigraph on page 51 is from the novel Jacob's Room, first published by Hogarth Press in 1922.

An iteration of Nikita and I (Cappadocia) was first published in Visual Verse Anthology VOL. 09 ~ CHAPTER 2.

My deepest gratitude:

To the editors of the publications in which some of these pieces had their first iterations.

To Ian Hooper for your constant guidance and unwavering support.

To Izzy Dempsey and Britt Wilson for so willingly helping me bring the cover to life.

To Isabelle Correa for your depth of insight and razor-sharp but honey-tipped editor's pen.

To the Villa Lena Foundation for your support in the final stretch.

To my family for so openly sharing our stories.

To my friends for the endless pep talks.

About the Author

Anja Mujić is a Bosnian/Australian writer, dance artist, musician, and yoga/meditation facilitator based in Berlin. Her work has appeared in the shortlist of the Born Writers Award 2022 and in publications such as Collateral, Humana Obscura, TravelMag, Visual Verse Anthology, Dancehouse Diaries, and Be In The Know Berlin. It has also been commissioned for exhibition, theatre, performance, and film. Her first collection of poetry, love letters to places... (Leschenault Press 2022), was a number 1 best seller in its pre-order period and has since been released in Kindle and audiobook forms.

www.ingramcontent.com/pod-product-compliance
Ingram Content Group UK Ltd.
Pitfield, Milton Keynes, MK11 3LW, UK
UKHW042000230426
12048UKWH00009B/455